healing in the family

edited by Paul F. Wilczak Ph. D.

ABBEY PRESS
St. Meinrad, Indiana 47577

The five chapters of this book originally appeared as articles in the *In-Depth* Series, "Healing in the Family," published in the September 1978 through January 1979 issues of *MARRIAGE and Family Living* magazine. They are here copyrighted as a collection in slightly revised form.

PHOTO CREDITS: Deborah Churan, Cover; Strix Pix, page 4-5, 49, 68, and 78; Robert Eckert, page 12; Bob Smith, page 28; Vivienne della Grotta, page 35; Lois Duncan, page 40; Wallowitch, page 54.

Library of Congress Card Number
79-53515
ISBN 0-87029-158-0

St. Meinrad, Indiana 47577

CONTENTS

STOP

Introduction

In May of 1978 the Catholic Bishops of the United States declared 1980 "The Year of the Family" and called for family life ministries and for the training and support of those involved. If this call is to be answered realistically and effectively, the nature of the family must be well understood. According to Catholic theology, grace builds upon nature, and ministry takes place when such building occurs with human cooperation and involvement. Healing is an important aspect of ministry, especially healing the relationships between people. The bishops have acknowledged this by recognizing a ministry to "hurting" families. But can hurting families be healed? If they can, what kind of healing do they need? And what happens when families are healed? These are questions which point toward the heart of ministry to families, a ministry of pastoral care.

They are also questions which are not the monopoly of the churches. Serious people in secular helping professions have been grappling with these questions for several decades. Some of their efforts and findings were summarized in a special report by *Newsweek* magazine (May 15, 1978). The churches are now raising such questions in a serious way and are talking about and contributing to work with families already in progress in the world at large. And this is very much in keeping with the meaning of the gospel. Jesus proclaimed the reign of God to be at hand. It is present in the world coming to life between people both within and beyond the churches. In a way, we Christians are called by the gospel to catch up with God who is ahead of us, working in hidden ways. But in order to do this, we must learn to think in new ways and to minister in new modes. Ministry to hurting families is just such a venture.

One of the breakthroughs which has prepared the Catholic Church for such a new ministerial venture is the growing awareness that ministry is not primarily to individuals. Ministry is always to and for communities. The sacraments are all communal in character and symbolism; we have only thought of them in individual terms. But they have always functioned as communal rituals expressing the meaning of the Church as a local and a worldwide community. But the Church is a community of grace comprised of smaller natural communities, i.e., families. That is why ministry to families can provide incisive examples of that crucial combination of nature and grace which renders credible the care of God for human beings.

The Church proclaims that God's care is always with us. That care can be most striking and appreciated when we are in deep pain and trouble. It is then that the salvation which heals can strike us with telling force, breaking the bonds of our complacency. In the essays which form this book, families in crisis, pain, and suffering will be a major concern. The authors are all well qualified in marital and family psychotherapy and counseling. They are largely representative of the perspective on healing called "family therapy." And their perspective unfolds a model of persons related in organic systems of interaction and mutual dependence. Their work in fact gives much support and credibility to the realism of St. Paul's assertion, "Now you are Christ's body, and each of you a limb or organ of it" (1 Cor 12, 27). For we are beginning to realize that we do not live as individual islands complete in ourselves. We are instead participants in natural social systems which allow us to know, interact, and create for the future. When these systems are infused with the Spirit of God, they become the Body of Christ. And the most natural of these systems infused with the Spirit is the family.

It is my hope that these essays will help you think of the family in new ways. They will suggest new ways to understand its troubles and its many needs for ministry. But they will also open paths to increased awareness of familiar strengths and creativity evoked by stress and severe challenge. It is my belief that these new ways point into the future, the future for humanity as well as the Church.

I mentioned the Bishop's meeting at the begining of this introduction. Two weeks after that meeting a national conference on family therapy was held in Milwaukee. At that conference the question was raised as to whose prerogative family therapy will be in the future. The psychiatrists? The psychologists? The social workers? The eminent family therapist Salvador Minuchin M.D. responded, "If family therapy is the prerogative of anyone, it is the prerogative of the religious healers, as it has been for hundreds of years." I believe his words have profound significance for ministers. But healing in the family is also the deep concern of all persons, for all of us have our roots in and draw our life from families. This book is an attempt to indicate some ways in which this concern can become a quest for healing.

But as a quest it will be incomplete and not fully satisfying. Greater depth will always be possible, always inviting us beyond the status quo. For the hurting family that finds relief from their pain is like the man stumbling across the treasure hidden in the field. They have experienced a new *event;* they have encountered real care in a new way. This implies a *reversal* of their usual way of life, a need to sell what they possess of the old way. And then there is the *decision*—to buy that field and to own that treasure. This simple parable reveals much about helping families who hurt. For putting aside the familiar ways of pain, hurt, insensitivity, blaming, avoidance, and irresponsibility means conversion to the deep yet daily living of our faith that God is love. For healing, as a good gift, comes from God. And to evoke, enhance, and celebrate this healing is ministry. Though the development of this ministry is incomplete and fragmentary, in it we can begin to comprehend the fullness of its source, He whom Jesus called our Father.

Paul F. Wilczak

I

The Family Seen as a System

Michael E. Kerr, M.D.

Michael E. Kerr M.D. is Clinical Assistant Professor and Director of Training, Georgetown University Family Center, Georgetown University Medical School. Dr. Kerr has written numerous articles and papers for periodicals, as well as chapters for books and videotape presentations. He is also in the private practice of family psychotherapy.

One of the most exciting recent developments in the understanding of human behavior has been the application of *systems thinking* to the study of the human family. This application has resulted in a new understanding of the origin of emotional, physical, and social problems and in more effective methods of treatment for these problems.

Development of Systems Thinking

Systems thinking contrasts with the prevailing model of thinking in medicine and psychiatry, namely the individual model. The individual model views illness as reflecting a defect or disturbance *within the symptomatic person.* The systems model views illness as reflecting a defect or disturbance *within the symptomatic person's important relationship system.* For most people, this important relationship system is the family.

Making this shift in understanding from an individual to a systems model is far more difficult than it might first appear. The systems model focuses on the *interdependence and mutual influencing* of the various parts that make up a system. We have little difficulty seeing this interdependence of parts when studying unemotional subjects from which we can be detached. An astronomer, for example, might beautifully describe the mutual influencing of the planets in the solar system where the movement of one planet cannot be adequately explained without understanding the movements of other planets. That same astronomer, however, may, in the more emotional environment of his family, begin blaming his wife for being the *cause* of their unhappiness. Had that astronomer maintained his systems perspective, he might have said to his wife, "We both react in highly emotional ways to each other and in doing so force ourselves into positions in which both of us are uncomfortable."

The more rapid development of systems thinking within the nonbehavioral sciences is probably related to the fact that we have more difficulty in thinking systems when studying ourselves than when studying subjects removed from us.

The stimulus for the development of systems thinking in the behavioral sciences came from the family movement in psychiatry and mental health. *General systems theory* had been developed prior to the family movement, but it was never a major influence on thinking in psychiatry.

The family movement began in the 1950s with researchers studying the families of emotionally disturbed patients in addition to the patients themselves. Many factors contributed to this shift in focus from individual to family, not the least of which was the observation that mentally ill patients would often improve in the hospital, only to deteriorate when they went home to their families. While there had long been an emotional undercurrent in psychiatric hospitals that blamed the families for making the patients sick, family researchers were trying to get beyond blame and to gain a better understanding of the interactive process between patient and family. In the back of every researcher's mind was the belief that a better understanding of family process could lead to more effective treatment methods.

This shift in focus from individual to family eventually *forced the development of new concepts* to explain what was being observed. The concepts that were developed to explain family interaction came to be know collectively as *family systems theory.*

Applying Systems Thinking to the Family

Applying systems theory to the family results in viewing the symptoms of a person as actually symptoms of a problem in the family. For example, instead of diagnosing the heavily drinking housewife as an alcoholic and defining her as the sick family member, using systems theory, her drinking is understood as being related to her *position of functioning* within the family relationship system. While all family members give in and adapt to each other, the drinking housewife is the one who has given in the most. Her repeated compromises to soothe family tensions have led to a buildup of tension that she attempts to deal with by excessive drinking. The family has usually come to view her drinking as the *cause* of the family's turmoil and has put increasing pressure on her to get her to stop. Anxious efforts to get her to stop drinking become an additional set of family expectations to which she tries to respond, and yet does not meet. This increases her disappointment in herself and drives her further towards compulsive and excessive drinking. It is an escalating emotional process in which all family members play their parts. To break the cycle requires at least one person in the family to focus more on his or her own part in the problem and to quit pressuring others to be different. Conceptualizing the problem this way does not ignore the fact that the wife does fall back on drinking to deal with stress and that to a certain extent her drinking creates a problem for others. This is her problem, but her drinking and its effects on others is only a part of the total problem in the family. Her drinking is *more a symptom* than a cause of a family problem.

The goal of the therapist who is working out of a systems theory is to help the family redefine the problem in a systems perspective, thereby gaining more options for doing something about it. A husband of a drinking wife, for example, need not wait for his wife to change as a solution to the situation. Once he accepts the fact that he has a part in the problem he can begin to work on himself.

Therapies such as psychoanalysis are based on the individual model and are often limited to the symptomatic person "wanting help." Family therapy is not limited in this way. From a systems perspective, any motivated family member can change the family by working *on changing self* and his or her own contribution to the problem. Disciplining one's own thinking to look past the symptom and concentrate on the background family emotional process is difficult. Most people and most mental health professionals focus on the symptomatic individual and treat him or her because that is where the problem appears to be. When the focus is placed on the family process, it is amazing how much breathing room individuals gain to think and work out their own problems.

The Bowen Theory

Murray Bowen, a psychiatrist who begun his research into the family and its interactions while at the National Institute of Mental Health in 1954, and who has continued that research at the Georgetown University School of Medicine since 1959, has developed the most detailed and comprehensive family systems theory.

Bowen conceptualizes the family as a system of opposing forces. When these forces are in balance, the family is in a state of equilibrium characterized by a basic stability in spite of chronic problems, and the absence of the development of any new problems. The problems believed to be influenced by the balance of forces within the family system include mental illness, physical illness, and various types of social acting-out, such as delinquent behavior. When the opposing forces in a family system are out of balance, a state of disequilibrium exists with new problems emerging and existing ones deteriorating. It is stress that puts the family system out of equilibrium; the disequilibrium reflects a failure of the family to deal with the stress.

An analogy of the heart and vascular system may be helpful in clarifying the relationships of symptoms to system equilibrium. The cardiovascular system functions with a fascinating balance of forces, among which are heart rate, strength of heart contraction, resistance in the blood vessels, oxygen requirements of the tissues, and a host of others. When these forces are in balance, a basic equilibrium known as homeostasis exists. A strong, healthy heart and vascular system has the reserve to withstand almost any kind of stress and still keep the system in balance and symptom free. If the heart or vascular system faces the stress of being moderately diseased, the body calls upon certain compensating mechanisms to maintain homeostasis. If the stress is great, the compensating mechanisms will be overloaded, the system will go out of balance, and symptoms will emerge: for example, congestion of fluid in the lungs leading to difficult breathing. When the stress diminishes, the symptoms will disappear and equilibrium will be restored. In the severely diseased or very weak heart, there is little reserve and the body's compensation mechanisms are not able to maintain equilibrium without chronic symptoms. When the impairment is severe, equilibrium can be maintained only when stress on the system is kept very low, for example, by the person spending most of the day lying in bed.

This analogy of the cardiovascular system can help us understand the family relationship system as theorized by Bowen. He has described two primary forces: a force towards *individuality* or differentiation and a force towards *togetherness* or fusion. When these forces are in balance, a state of equilibrium exists. When they are out of balance, the family is in disequilibrium. Like the body, the family has compensating or adaptive mechanisms to preserve equilibrium when it is under stress, but when these mechanisms are overloaded or fail, symptoms develop that are related to the type of mechanisms the family has employed to preserve homeostasis.

The togetherness or fusion force is rooted deep in our biological makeup and is presumably a force that also operates in nonhuman species. This togetherness force is the glue or binding of our relationships and accounts for the way people function together in a system. Togetherness or fusion is reflected in our need for and investment in others. Sensitivity to disapproval, criticism, rejection, and where one fits in the hierarchy of social structuring is all part of the fusion force. Togetherness is reflected in sympathetic reactions to the plight of others and a feeling of *responsibility for* the functioning and well-being of others. It is a force that overrides autonomy and leads to a dissolution of individual boundaries. The fusion force is a leveling force, a force towards sameness. It is reflected in an intolerance for differences in thinking within a group.

The individuality or differentiation force is

presumably also rooted deep in our biological makeup and operates in some form in nonhuman species. Individuality refers to the need for each person to be himself or herself. It is reflected in an ability to be involved with others and still maintain autonomy. Functioning based on differentiation does not assume *responsibility for* others, but will reflect *responsibility to* others. Individuality describes a capacity to avoid being emotionally influenced by disapproval, criticism, or threats of rejection. Individuality is reflected in an ability to act on one's thinking and beliefs even in the midst of highly emotional reactions by the family or social group. By not being based on winning approval or acceptance, individuality is reflected in the willingness to live with the anxiety of the moment in order to gain a long-term solution to a problem.

With these differentiation and fusion forces in mind, one can study families and observe how they differ in the relative influences of individuality and togetherness. Some families are more fused than others; and in some families, members operate in a more differentiated way than in others. There appears to be an optimum balance of individuality and togetherness in families and social groups just as there is an optimum balance of forces in the cardiovascular system. When this optimum balance exists in a family, it is strong, healthy, and does not rely heavily on compensatory mechanisms to maintain equilibrium. The family is, therefore, able to cope with significant amounts of stress without developing symptoms.

From clinical and research experience, it can be said that families in the most serious difficulty are those in which the fusion or togetherness force begins to dominate family activity and in which individuality has become a scarce commodity. People in these strongly fused families are feeling at one and the same time a greater need for each other in order to function and a corresponding greater sense of pressure or encroachment from each other. They place more emotional demands on each other than in a less fused family. This excessive need for each other generates anxiety within the family system. The anxiety is chronic and requires compensating family mechanisms to deal with it. Like the heart, the more these compensating mechanisms are called into action, the less reserve in the system and the more vulnerable it becomes to the development of symptoms under added stress. As mentioned, these symptoms can be mental illness, physical illness, social acting out, or family conflict and disruption.

Some families are more fused than others and the greater this fusion, the greater the family's vulnerability to the development of problems. The emergence of these problems depends on the level of stress in the system.

The fact that some families have the togetherness force in better balance than others is a product of the emotional process in families over the generations. The evolution of this emotional process through generations is highly complex, but, simply stated, highly fused families tend to produce children with the same togetherness tendency who then marry people like themselves. If you trace a family over many generations, some units will show increasing fusion, while others will show some decrease in fusion. This latter process of decreasing fusion is related to the fact that some children are left out of the intensity of the emotional process in their families and leave home somewhat better differentiated than their parents. They, then, marry people like themselves.

When the fusion process builds to the extreme across generations, the end results are multiproblem families with increased incidences of physical and emotional illness, social acting out, and fragmentation. Even these most fused families can be stabilized if the conditions are ideal. One of the most important conditions is the degree to which the family has maintained meaningful emotional contact with its extended family system. It has been a repeated clinical observation that the greater the emotional cutoff from the past, the greater the tendency for problems in the nuclear family unit. This observation has led to the establishment of one of the most important principles of family therapy: reestablishment of emotional contact with the extended family can significantly reduce the problems of the family seeking therapy. Meaningful emotional contact does not mean people simply living near each other. People three thousand miles apart can be in better emotional contact than people living in the same house.

In addition to basic differences between families in the balance of individuality and togetherness forces over the generations, there are also fluctuations in this balance within the same family over time. These fluctuations are related to the level of anxiety in the family system at any given moment. When anxiety increases, there is an increase in activity geared toward family togetherness and a consequent increase in the use of compensatory mechanisms for dealing with the anxiety generated by too much closeness. These shifts in balance are most dramatic in poorly differentiated family systems, but do occur, to some extent, in all families when there's stress.

The Role of Anxiety

Stress and anxiety are words that need further definition in the understanding of family systems theory. Stress can be any event that has the potential for generating anxiety in a person, family, or social group. Anxiety is the person's reaction to the event. In the earlier discussion of individuality and togetherness forces, these were described as having roots in human biological makeup. Anxiety is also a biological response. The understanding of anxiety is meant to be broad enough to include anxious states of whales, birds, insects, and even one-celled animals. So the word anxiety as used here is intended to convey more than is usually meant by statements such as "I feel anxious." It is conceptualized as a more basic phenomenon.

Anxiety has a very definite and tangible effect on relationship systems. Anxious systems behave quite differently from calm ones. As mentioned earlier, when anxiety increases, motion toward togetherness also increases. Take for example a wife who for one reason or another begins to feel anxious. This increased anxiety will likely accentuate her felt need for closeness or togetherness. As she moves towards her husband for satisfaction of that need, he may respond in a differentiated way, by calmly dealing with that need in his wife, which in turn satisfies it and reduces her anxiety. He may, however, react to his wife's anxiety by anxiously withdrawing from what he feels is a demand or encroachment on himself. His withdrawal is a mechanism for dealing with the anxiety generated by too much closeness. The husband's withdrawal leaves the wife with an increased sense of isolation, more anxiety, and an even greater desire for closeness. A more differentiated response on her part, at this point, would be to recognize the cycle, tone down her need and anxiety, and not pressure her mate for a response. But if both husband and wife begin anxiously reacting to each other, an escalating cycle develops which leaves the wife feeling quite uncomfortable and often appearing as if she is the one with the problem. In fact, the actual problem is the level of anxiety and lack of differentiation in both partners. When the anxiety decreases, the cycle will *automatically* reverse.

It is important to keep in mind that the problems in an anxious system are in many ways products of the mechanisms designed to deal with that anxiety. In the case just described, the wife continues to seek comfort through closeness while the husband seeks to protect himself through distance. This process has gone beyond the point where it is any way helpful. This is characteristic of an anxious system, i.e., people's attempts to deal with the problem actually create more of a problem. What is really helpful is a reduction of anxiety and not more fusion or togetherness determined activity. Compensatory mechanisms like distance do help stabilize a system up to a point, but eventually, as in the impaired cardiovascular system, the mechanisms can become the problem.

In anxious families, people are battling over many issues, believing a problem will be solved by settling an issue. The issue is not the problem. The underlying emotional reactions and interactions of family members are the obstacles that prevent families from finding solutions.

The Value of a Systems Perspective

Clinical and research experience with Bowen's family systems theory now exceeds twenty years. In that time it has been well established that while both individuality and togetherness forces are equally essential in the balance of a family system, the more a system evolves towards differentiation, the better for the system and all its members. A family weighted in the balance towards individuality, experiences less chronic anxiety, has more reserve under stress, and is comprised of physically and mentally healthier people than in more fused systems.

Establishment of the fact that differentiation is healthy for the system has led to a new form of psychotherapy. The difference is such that mental health professionals who use systems theory in their practice are reluctant to even call it therapy. Systems "therapy" revolves around one or more motivated family members trying to improve their ability to function by focusing on differentiation as opposed to fusion or togetherness. It is a long term and gradual process, but its value is that one person's change can favorably influence the entire family system. Many special techniques that cannot be detailed here are involved in this process. One of the most important has been to assist the individual in studying the multigenerational emotional process within one's own family. Such an effort is necessarily long-term because emotional bias about one's own family does not change quickly. Overly idealized and/or overly critical views about other family members are so deeply ingrained in all of us, that to change these views is no simple task. It can be done, however, when people work on their emotional reactiveness, try to be objective, and get beyond excessive blaming of self or others. To accomplish this, a person must come to know and respect the individuality of others in the family.

The value of systems thinking on a societal level remains to be seen. One person, working on his or her own differentiation, can influence an entire family, but, obviously, not an entire society. But systems thinking has opened the door to new ways of conceptualizing social problems and offers promise for favorably influencing continued human development.

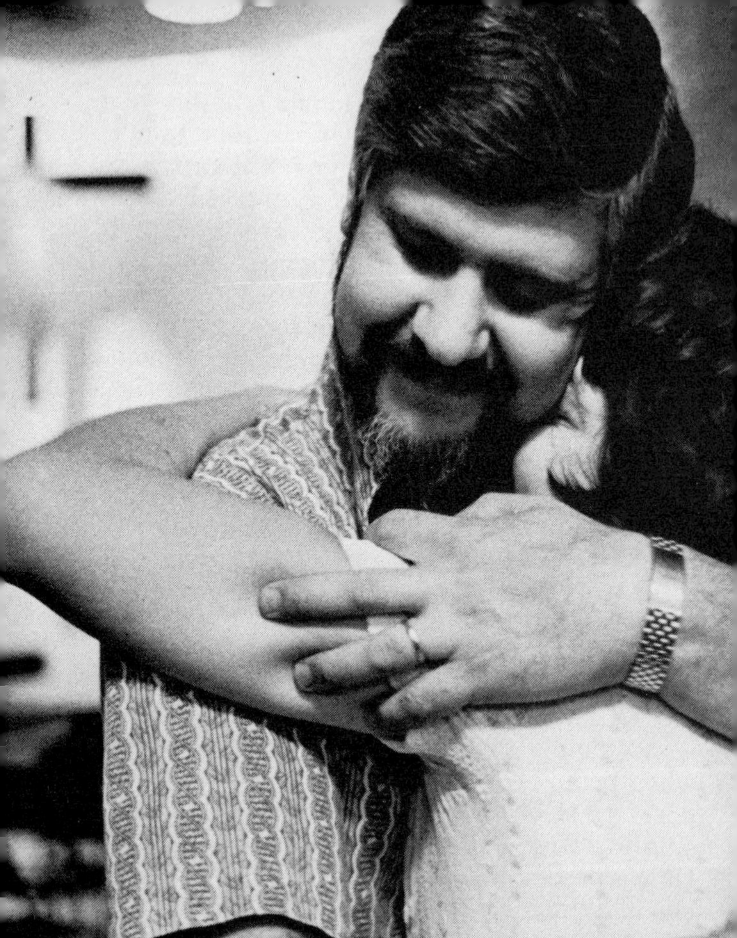

II

The Role of Celebrant in Family Therapy

Andrew F. Bambrick

Fr. Andrew F. Bambrick is a teaching chaplain at Allentown (PA) State Hospital. He is a supervisor in the American Association of Marriage and Family Therapists. For the past six years he has been Co-Director of Training on a Family Therapy Research Project at Lehigh University. He is Departments' Editor on the International Journal of Family Therapy.

Families have roots and common experiences. A family may be seen as a group with its own bundle of values derived in large measure from institutions in which it claims membership, such as church, civic associations, and neighborhood affiliations which flesh out its particular identity.

Our family name is like an envelope which identifies who we are and those who are nearest to us. Consciousness, values, and patterns of relating are formed within the context of our family. It is there that we learn that we, as well as others, matter. Our values and patterns of relating are what make us interlock with other family members.

These values and patterns are especially noticeable as the family attempts to resolve conflicts. Broadly speaking, family conflicts may be between husband and wife, between parents and children, between the family and the community. A value is an *attitude* or a way of evaluating events that typifies a person or a group. Two dominant types of values are expressed in families: "continuous" values and "discontinuous" values.

Continuous values are those which espouse the goodness of compassion, justice, equality, and relatedness. Discontinuous values are those which espouse the goodness of systems of controls, of rational approaches to problems, of law and legal codes, of orderly procedures and discipline.

For example, a husband and wife may argue over the appropriateness of their daughter dating a school dropout. The wife may accuse the husband of being distant, cold, and uninvolved in the future of their daughter. The husband may accuse the wife of being overly involved and sentimental. In this case, the husband espouses discontinuous values by affirming the need for the goodness of control and discipline, while the wife, on the other hand, affirms the need for goodness and emphasizes the uniqueness of her daughter's situation.

Unsuccessful attempts to resolve this situation, or situations like this, tend to foster destructive patterns. These patterns include scapegoating, silencing, speaking for one another, and cliques. The presence of these patterns within a family causes pain, uncertainty, and disorganization, which often lead families to seek therapy. Families enter therapy with some fears, reservations, and hopes. One family member may say to herself, "Is there something wrong with all of us? Is that why we were asked to come in? What is this family therapy anyway?"

Perhaps the basic premise behind family therapy is that a healing relationship is rightfully found between those who are related and relating. Family healing connotes that there are certain restorative and creative potentials in a family gathering. These potentials are provided by God to help the family come to terms with who they are, what they have become, and where they are going.

The religious minister as family therapist is in a unique position to provide conditions which facilitate reconciliation and is often able to go beyond that. As in the examples below, by introducing the thrust of discontinuous values (reason) into situations devoid of it, or by inserting the theme of continuous values (sympathy) into situations devoid of this thrust, he or she can at times activate the reconciliation process.

Troubled Christian families tend to think of a religious minister, acting as family therapist, as a representative of God. They feel that the resolution of their conflict should take place in an atmosphere which fosters reconciliation, respect for individual differences, and an ultimate dependence on God.

In the "Go-Between Process" of family therapy, developed by Dr. Gerald Zuk, one of the pioneers in family therapy at Eastern Pennsylvania Psychiatric Institute, the family therapist has three roles: the role of go-between, the role of side-taker, and the role of celebrant.

In the role of go-between the religious minister/family therapist focuses on issues where the family members are in conflict. The minister/therapist attempts to encourage them to be open to themselves and to the presence of God in their midst. He or she sets limits or rules out certain behavior during the discussion of the conflict.

As side-taker, the religious minister/therapist directly supports the position of a family member, in order to shift or reduce the destructive patterns of relating, and spells out why he or she is siding with this person at this time and the reasons for such a decision. As side-taker and mediator, the religious minister/therapist attempts to break a family's deadlock by interjecting continuous or discontinuous values, as needed to foster reconciliation as well as independence.

The religious minister/therapist is asked to assume another role as well, by being put in a position of "certifying" that something has happened or is about to happen that is important to the family. Thereby, the minister/therapist is cast in the role of celebrant.

A celebrant is a person who is invested with the mantle of an important institution in the community. The doctor, judge, minister, policeman, politician, and teacher are institutional authority figures and, as such, are empowered by society to seal and label steps and changes in individuals and society.

The religious minister/therapist is called upon to officially accept, to "certify" a change that may be in progress or has already occurred in a family. The greater the disorganization of the family, the more likely the therapist may be perceived as celebrant. The role of celebrant is most applicable with blue collar, poverty families, and families interviewed at the point of crisis. The role is diminished as the intensity of emotions and the disorganization within the family subside.

The following vignettes describe how the therapist used the role of celebrant in working with families.

CASE I

Ralph, the father, is in his midforties. He has a husky build and deep set eyes. For the past eighteen years, he has been employed by the local steel mill. During the family therapy sessions, he communicates more nonverbally than verbally. Alice, the mother, is in her midthirties. She is small in stature and overweight. Two days a week she is employed as a seamstress for a dress factory. She has a tendency to speak for the rest of the family. Susan is seventeen. She is bright, cheerful, a straight A student in school. Margaret is fifteen. She is slightly overweight, sensitive. At present she is carrying two failure notices—one in English and the other in math. Ralph Jr. is eleven years old and the youngest in the family. He is a chunky boy with red cheeks. During the family sessions, it becomes evident that he simply wants all the hurt and pain to go away. The woman therapist is an ordained minister in the United Church of Christ.

In the past, this family's approach to problem solution could only be expressed in terms of "might makes right." Presently this approach isn't working. The family is so involved in applying the pressure of rules in order to solve its problems with Margaret, that it makes little use, if any, of compassion, warmth, and support.

During the past few weeks, conflict has es-

calated in the family. Last week Margaret ran away from home for three days. Upon returning, she refused to answer questions as to her whereabouts. Up to this point, the parents could not admit that their daughter's behavior called for compassion, warmth, and support as well as disapproval. They simply scapegoated Margaret. In their view, she was entitled to her position, but she was wrong.

At the family session, the mother's eyes were swollen from crying, the father's face was drawn and haggard. Susan sat quietly with a puzzled look on her face. Ralph Jr. was preoccupied in rubbing out a nonexistent spot from the arm of his chair.

At this point, the therapist called upon all family members to treat Margaret with warmth and compassion, to express their joy that she who had run away had returned. "Now is the time for forgiveness and celebration."

Slowly the mother rose and hugged Margaret and said, "Oh Margaret, we love you." Her father said, "I'm glad you are back with us." Then he hugged her also. The faces of Susan and Ralph Jr. beamed with joy. They completed the pattern of family healing by embracing their sister and telling her how good it was to have her back.

In this situation where the family was debilitated by a preoccupation with the values of order, the therapist, as celebrant, espoused the goodness of compassion, thereby activating creative potentials within the family, so healing could take place. She could then celebrate the fact that God was in their midst and that their embracing was a sign of reconciliation.

CASE II

Jim and Alice have been married four years. Alice is thirty-six years old and a homemaker. She has three children from a previous marriage. Jim is thiry-seven and a mid-level executive who spends a great deal of time away from home. The children are Joe, fifteen, Nancy, thirteen, and John, eleven. Their therapist is a Catholic priest. During the past few weeks there has been a lot of bickering and fighting going on in the family.

After Alice's divorce from her former husband, Ted, she decided that she would give all that she could to her children to make up for the divorce over which she felt some guilt. While dating Alice, Jim decided that what the children needed was warmth and support. Jim and Alice both came from families who encouraged them to overgive.

Fighting broke out just after the children visited their father, Ted. He had taken the children skiing and to Disneyworld, gave them extra desserts, and let them stay up as late as they wanted.

Upon returning home, the children state that Ted is the greatest. In many ways they demonstrate their preference for Ted over Alice and Jim. Alice is angry, but she tries to give the children more and more things. Jim feels like an outsider with the family. He fears that disciplining the children will cause Alice and the children to dislike him

Jim and Alice are acting as though, when it comes to relating to the children, compassion and warmth are all that is needed. The children state that they feel that Jim and Alice are trying to buy them off. After several sessions, definite patterns begin to emerge.

Whenever the family attempts to negotiate needs and set limits, chaos erupts. The pattern is as follows. Alice speaks first, Jim looks to Alice before he speaks. Joe says he isn't getting attention. Nancy distracts herself by staring at the floor, and John nods in agreement with his brother and says, "I know you don't care about us." The pattern is clear. Alice is the initiator, Jim follows, Joe is the opposer, Nancy is silent, and John is in coalition with his brother, Joe.

The therapist, at this point, intervenes and says, "You are all trying to help. However, you are using your love destructively. Your way of relating causes pain and disorganization. At the end of your discussion, things still remain unclear."

In this situation the therapist lets it be known, "certifies," that this particular pattern used by the family is destructive. In this he assumes the role that I call that of the "celebrant." He also confronts the family with the overlooked value of orderly process and affirms the notion that a sense of order must be achieved if this family is going to profit from their relating, negotiating, and attempts to heal one another.

The role of the celebrant is a new role which has emerged in the field of family therapy. The major function of celebrant, here described, is to bring to an occasion of "healing-change" the assuring social recognition and acceptance of it by a person respected for his or her commitment to ultimate values.

All three roles in the Go-Between Process readily accomodate themselves to pastoral usage. Hopefully many more priests, religious, ministers, and dedicated believers will become more involved in ministering to "hurting families."

III

Family Systems Therapy: A Path to Coping

Patricia Hanes Meyer

Patricia Hanes Meyer is a Clinical Instructor in the Department of Psychiatry at Georgetown University Family Center. She has also served as an Advisory Editor of The Family *and has contributed to* MARRIAGE and Family Living's *"Talking with Someone Else"* *column.*

Since the 1950s, interest in "family therapy" has been on the rise. Those involved in it saw it at first give rise to concepts and methods of dealing with problem behavior on the part of a member within the family, and then, the more ardent among them, by the 1970s, went on to see in it the best way of dealing with almost any human behavioral problem. At the root of this shift in theory and method of treatment, was the seminal work of several different psychotherapists. The differences among these leaders is evident in the techniques derived from them as practiced in family therapy today. One of these pioneers is Murray Bowen, M.D.

Dr. Bowen began his psychoanalytically oriented research into family dynamics in the late 1940s. By the mid-1950s, a distinctive theory of the family began to develop as a result of the work he carried out at the National Institute of Mental Health. In his research, entire families of schizophrenic patients were hospitalized at NIMH, where they lived together on the ward, and their interactions were observed and studied. In 1959, the NIMH research project came to an end and Dr. Bowen moved to Georgetown University Medical Center. At Georgetown, Dr. Bowen developed what has come to be known as the "Bowen Family Systems Theory" and a psychotherapy of "coaching" based upon it. Dr. Bowen's current research focuses upon the inter-relationships of the emotional processes of families and of society at large.

The Bowen Theory

The Bowen Theory is comprised of eight interrelated concepts. To do them justice in such a brief essay is not possible. I have chosen instead to discuss several of the main principles and ideas of the theory along with two examples of families who were "coached" in resolving family problems in accordance with Bowen's theory.

Bowen's theory assumes the existence of an interconnectedness in the behavior of different people through emotional ties. This means simply that the interaction of two or more people (a family, a group, or a set of coworkers) is, in fact, inflenced by the emotional ties between them—how important they are to each other, what their mutual expectations are, how they depend or rely upon each other, and so on. Among relationships with emotional ties, those within the family certainly are the most significant.

Every person is born into the web of an emotional system. For instance, a firstborn child is greeted with numerous spoken and unspoken expectations from the parents. His or her formidable six or eight pounds do not give rise to such expectations, but rather such expectations find their source in the negative or positive feelings that each parent carries from experiences within his or her own family of origin. Hence, the infant has joined a family in which she may be the catalyst for her mother's finally gaining a sense of role in life, or his dad's competitor for the attention of mother, or a replacement for the parents with whom his mother now has little contact. The manner in which these parents invest their emotions in their relationship to their baby and seek return in their own emotional satisfaction from the infant will determine, at least in part, to what degree the child will grow into an independent, self-motivated, responsible person.

It will be this basic foundation of independence or dependence that will govern, to a large degree, the quality of *emotional reactivity* in relationships which the person will experience. For instance, in the adolescent period when peer pressure is such a powerful force, two children with opposite ratios of *self-responsibility* (connoting a high degree of chosen self-direction in manner) to *emotional reactivity* (connoting a high degree of predetermination in manner) will handle such pressure differently. The one with more reactivity and less self-responsibility will be more easily swayed by threats of disapproval from peers and may easily succumb to promises of approval. The adolescent with a substantial amount of self-responsibility and less reactivity will be aware of these same pulls from significant peers but will be able to define for him- or herself what behavior to follow even with the outcome resulting in momentary disapproval.

Each of these two adolescents will seek and choose mates who are similiar in self-responsibility and reactivity. The couple with lower self-clarity will be more vulnerable to the forces of peer pressure and anxiety in life and may form life decisions in concert with such forces. In raising their children, their foundation of lesser self-belief and the greater influence of others will come into play when children's behavior and activity place the parents in the difficult position of walking the line between self-belief and "what others expect you to do." So, too, will emotional patterns come into play in the relationship between the spouses, as they handle the many tensions and pressures which surface in every marriage.

The Impact Of Stress on Families

Any family unit, if put under enough prolonged stress, will develop *dysfunction.* Such dysfunction will appear as a breakdown in social, emotional, or physical functioning. Examples of breakdown in social functioning are alcoholism in a parent and delinquency in a child. A marriage may remain intact with the children doing okay, while one parent becomes incapacitated through alcohol. Emotional dysfunctioning would be seen, for instance, in severe depression in a family member while the children and the marital relationship remain in satisfactory shape. Physical dysfunction would be seen in a family member developing a chronic illness. Some families show all three forms of dysfunction, others two, and yet other families experience only one.

Different families will have differing degrees of basic emotional reactivity to stress and this will determine, at least in part, how serious and debilitating the problems will be for the family. The quantity, duration, and severity of symptoms in a family reflect the degree of reactivity in the family.

That a family is a connected system can be seen in clinical cases again and again when pressure in one part of the system creates a reaction in another part of the system often without the awareness of the family member. For instance, illness in an aging parent may make adult children tense and worried, resulting in these adults being less calm, less effective, and more argumentative with their own children. Such tension between parent and adolescent may be expressed by the parents in terms of "What's gotten into that kid of ours?" while the adolescent may be thinking, "Mom has been on my back lately." In this way each family member reacts to the other. Such tension may give rise to a rift between the generations without any awareness of the forces at work (one being worry about the aging parent) within the family.

The Impact of Social Forces on the Family

Vulnerability in terms of reactivity is heightened in our contemporary world by numerous factors, four of which will be mentioned here.

1. Humans, for the first time in history, face a population explosion which, in turn,

threatens a depletion of natural resources as evidenced through oil shortages, water shortages, and electrical blackouts.

2. The rushed, frantic, and chaotic pace of modern life pressures many into letting some things go without dealing with them—often resulting in the evasion of very real problems.

3. Parental attitudes as well as modern appliances, which make it possible for a motivated mother to do all of the housework herself, have deprived children of a significant role in the family. Children find themselves leading a life of school, snacks, TV, and the like without making any consistent contribution to the family in which they are forming the emotional identity with which they will enter the adult world.

4. Finally, people today have lost a part of their sense of belongings to larger families—aunts, uncles, grandparents, cousins. When adults live thousands of miles from their parents, maintaining contact and responding to life occurences in extended family is all but impossible. The overall impact results in a reduced sense of the heritage which one has to hand on to one's children.

These societal shifts have brought about a world in which adults have *less awareness of and self-confidence in* what they themselves believe about important issues, and as a consequence, they rely more on experts to tell them how to live. Guidance is sought on how to garden, how to succeed in marital intimacy, how to raise children, etc. Overdependency on experts is highly symptomatic.

The Bowen theory has emphasized that

every person's ability to successfully maintain a responsible and productive life unburdened by chronic severe problems is connected to the quality and amount of person-to-person relating which each person experiences with those who are emotionally most significant—the nuclear and extended family. Further, the quality and degree of this emotional relationship with one's family of origin will constitute the foundation with which a person moves into adult life—capable of responding by choice to challenges as a person rather than merely reacting to the pressures of peers. In each case where a person is reactive to another by avoidance of that other, the emotional connection between those persons is affected and emotional satisfaction is diminished.

Family Therapy Based upon Bowen Theory

For Bowen therapy to be successful, a person has to be willing to work toward a thorough understanding of how a problem came to be in the first place and what various factors have played a part in it. The person who can become this objective about an emotional problem will find a new capacity to begin to change self in relation to the problem. If a person in the emotional system can accomplish this change, the family system of reactivity will be altered and the symptomatic problem will decrease significantly or disappear entirely. Two examples might make this clear.

In one family, a mother and father came for "coaching" out of concern for their fourteen-year-old daughter Sandy, who was acting rebel-

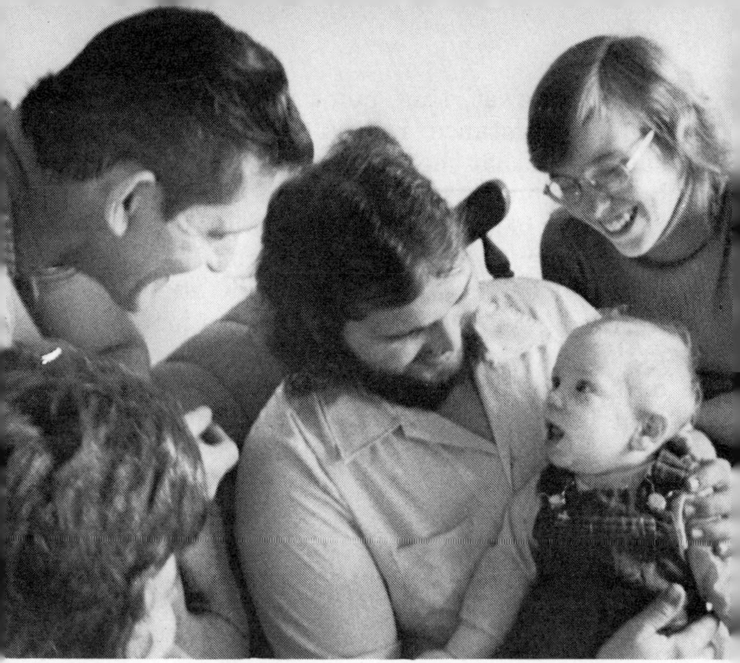

liously and doing poorly in school.

The parents had experienced fair success with their older children; they had been consistent in making rules and enforcing them. With this youngest child, however, neither parent seemed able to be consistent nor to follow through on established rules or punishments. It was as if the demands and moods of this child kept her parents confused and unsure that their responses were indeed the right ones. As a consequence, Sandy had grown up being treated differently than the others and each member of the family had come to view her a bit protectively. By fourteen, she had developed some rebellious behavior including experimentation with drugs and unsatisfactory performance at school.

It was at this point that the parents sought assistance. It was not until many sessions later that the mother and father began to be clear about what, in fact, had been going on for many years. They began to see that rules had frequently been given out and then, under pressure or as a result of doubt about their fairness, revoked. There had been a long history of treating young Sandy differently than the others. Each parent began to see how each had contributed to this way of dealing with Sandy and had brought about her reaction.

In order to change this reaction pattern, the parents were coached to consider a new course of action—to permit Sandy to make more decisions but at the price of facing the consequences without being shielded from them. At first, Sandy was understandably furious, as her parents began to demonstrate their determination to allow her to experience the outcomes of her choices. For instance: Sandy was told that by agreement with her boyfriend's parents, any evidence of her continuing to smoke marijuana would be shared with them, since they disapproved of their son's dating anyone who did. New evidence came to light and was shared as agreed upon.

As Sandy's parents began to follow through again and again, she began to realize that no longer would she be treated as a "special member of the family" who did not have to follow the rules of the house as the others did and that if she chose to behave irresponsibly, it was likely that she would face some uncomfortable moments in the future.

Sandy's family has not solved all of its

problems, and for it to do so will require yet more work and effort with the coaching. However, they have managed to allow Sandy to grow up and to face being a future adult with the same expectations and ground rules which have governed this development in their older children. Sandy's reaction? Well, with little thanks nor appreciation (yet) for her parents' shift in relating to her, she has assumed a more responsible life-style; her grades are better, and rebellious behavior is rarely present anymore.

In another instance, the person seeking coaching was the wife in a family with two boys. As is often the case, the complaint which brought Mrs. Collins in concerned her son, but the most upsetting relationship in the family was between herself and her husband. From the onset of the lengthy marriage, Mrs. Collins, who was the only child of a demanding mother, had assumed a relationship with her husband in which she attempted to please him. The problem was that in order to please her husband, she often behaved differently than she thought she should. But having done so, she recieved little satisfaction, for her husband rarely approved of her attempt. Needless to say, Mrs. Collins had assumed a life stance of frustration and was rather hopeless that much of her life could be different.

Coaching with Mrs. Collins shifted almost immediately from her son Tom to her own life dissatisfactions, particularly to her way of relating to her husband. It was clear that, until she was more satisfied in her marriage, it would be difficult for her to begin to be more effective with her son.

First, Mrs. Collins put her effort into trying to understand why she continually undervalued her own opinions in making decisions in the family and overvalued her husband's. At the same time, she began to take a look at her difficulty in experiencing angry disapproval from her husband and others as well. It was as if she was so uncomfortable with disapproval that she would forego her own opinion about how she should handle a child or a problem rather than risk facing it. The result of both of these tendencies was a sense of depression and the feeling that she was rather inferior.

Before Mrs. Collins was able to make much change in her participation in the family, it was necessary for her to begin to understand what her growing-up experience had been and the way in which she had related to each of her parents and they to her. From this insight, she was able to see the pattern of her actions with both her spouse and children in a context which helped make them understandable.

With the conviction arising from this understanding, Mrs. Collins found the determination to begin to redefine her relationship with both son and husband. With her husband, Mrs. Collins began to say and do what she felt she should do and prepared herself for the predictable anger that would follow. Such effort was easier than she expected, for Mr. Collins seemed as bewildered as he was angry. His behavior towards Mrs. Collins became more respectful and a little less demanding. From this initial success, Mrs. Collins found herself with more energy for parenting tasks. She was able for the first time to resist the debates with her son from which she never emerged a winner.

In summary, coaching families from a Bowen family theory orientation has meant working with the motivated member of the family who is distressed enough to do something about it. The effort moves from assisting the involved family members to begin to objectively understand the problem that brought them in—in the context of the growing-up experience of each—to assisting the family members to define for themselves ways of relating that would be more productive and personally satisfying.

IV

Family Oriented Therapy of Homosexual Behavior

Alfred A. Messer

Alfred A. Messer M.D. is an attending psychiatrist at a hospital in Atlanta, GA. An author of two books and numerous magazine and journal articles, Dr. Messer is consultant and moderator of a radio program, "Call the Psychiatrist."

How successful therapists are in treating the homosexual patient and helping him progress toward heterosexual relationships depends mainly on the patients motivation for seeking help. The individual who feels his sexual preference denies him family ties and a sense of posterity through marriage and children, or who feels inadequacy, shame, or humiliation, would be more likely to seek reorientation toward heterosexuality. The more homosexuality is considered an alternate life-style rather than a deviation, the less likely will persons seek treatment and the more difficult the therapy. As a therapist, I believe we must take issue with civil libertarians and elected officials who equate "gay rights" with "civil rights," and who insist that homosexuality represents an "orientation difference" rather than a deviation.

Traditional psychoanalysis of homosexuality was oriented toward analyzing one individual and involved, as a major element in therapy, a reliving of infantile experiences. Male homosexuality was viewed as the phobic avoidance of the female genitals, and treatment could proceed as for any phobia. This psychoanalytic view of male homosexual behavior as originating in a fear of castration has been modified as we have better understood nonsexual motivations in homosexual encounters which satisfy dependency or power needs (pseudohomosexuality). In this article, homosexual behavior is presented as a symptom of underlying family disorder and therefore amenable to combined individual and family treatment. By treating two (or preferably three) generations in one family together, therapists can clarify how the individual's sexual orientation arose *within* that family constellation.

Consider, for example, John Brooks, a nineteen-year-old student who was referrred to a psychiatrist by his parents in order "that something be done about his homosexuality." The family had known of the boy's homosexual behavior for three years but just recently became uncomfortable about it. John, an only child, was unconcerned; he enjoyed his way of life.

When the psychiatrist asked John whether there were any problems he did want help with, he said that he sometimes let himself be influenced by his homosexual friends to behave in an immature manner—staying out all night, driving wildly and nosily in rented cars, and phoning strangers collect in the middle of the night.

John was willing to begin therapy to improve his social relationships, but reiterated that he had no desire to do anything about his homosexual behavior. He answered all the psychiatrist's questions readily and was invited to return with his family.

When the family arrived for a joint session, the three were accompanied by a large German shepherd that lay protectively at the mother's side. Mr. Brooks owned several farms outside the county seat where they lived, served as a municipal judge, and was one of the town's leading citizens. The wife and son testified as to the father's business success and civic importance. He was a massive man, well over six feet tall, and wore horn-rimmed glasses. His hair was slicked back with a patent leather look, and he spoke in deep, sonorous tones, dropping names of U.S. Senators he felt free to call upon whenever he needed them. Mrs. Brooks was generally quiet and reticent during the interview, but occasionally there was a caustic outburst when she disagreed with her husband. She stated several times that all she cared about was having peace in the family; she had been raised in a home with a tyrannical and overbearing father and said, "I've seen enough family arguing to last a lifetime."

John's mother worried constantly about her son and had always been very protective of him. As a youngster, he had periodic attacks of asthma and bronchitis and she carried him around physically while she tended to household chores. He was fearful when he started school and stayed home many days at the beginning of the first year. The principal was concerned about the boy developing a school phobia. During those days when he stayed home, John and his mother played many games together and she taught him piano. He became an average student in grade and high school and was now a second-year student at a liberal arts college. When John first went off to college, his mother drove him there and spent an afternoon helping him get settled. He called home once a week and rarely talked with his father, but he and his mother would review all his activities.

During the first interview, it was evident that the husband carried on extramarital activities, both in town and on business trips. The wife hinted that she knew about these affairs, but what he did away from home was "his business." Nevertheless, the barbs she aimed at him were clearly indicative of her anger. When the psychiatrist questioned the husband further about his personal life, he was evasive and resorted to talking about his accomplishments and his important acquaintances. He did state, however, that in his home, his mother had been the dominant parent. When the relationship between John and his father was brought up again, the older man went back to talking about his own achievements. At no time did he give John any credit or reassurance in his attempts at being independent or assertive.

It was apparent that the father felt inadequate in his masculine role and could tolerate no challenge to his position, not even by his own son. Accordingly, any attempt toward masculinity on the part of the boy was thwarted. The father was abetted in this goal by his wife who kept the boy close to home and raised him in a "sissyish" fashion. She did not want another aggressive male in her environment.

When John was interviewed in an individual session, he could not recall any sexual interest or curiosity in his early life. He recalled being carried around by his mother, and being teased by his father because of this. He had no memory of self-stimulation and recalled no games of doctor and nurse with girls. When he was an adolescent, he was aware of sexual feelings, but he tried to push these feelings aside.

The initial impression was that John's fear of heterosexual activity, and of women in general, came from two sources: a) as a child and adolescent, sensual and sexual feelings were associated with physical contact with his mother and were burdened with guilt and therefore unacceptable; b) he felt women were overpowering and domineering and would annihilate or castrate men. Moreover, in John's family situation, whenever he attempted to assert himself in any area of life, including sexual curiosity, he was challenged rather than supported by his father.

At a subsequent family interview, the father gruffly mentioned the amount of money he had expended to give John every opportunity for education and travel. The father could not understand why his son was not functioning in life as family tradition dictated. The therapist noted the father seemed to respond primarily in a way detrimental to his son's self-image. Futher, before the mother or John said anything in the interview, they looked to the father for a cue that their statements were acceptable.

At the end of that session, the father expressed reluctance to return to treatment because he felt the therapy was pointless. The therapist solicited the mother's and son's reactions. Both felt that it would be useful for the family to work together on family problems, not solely on John's sexual orientation. The therapist then explained to the father that the son's problems could be a reflection of the lack of harmony within the family, and since the father was a key member of the family unit, he would have to be a part of the treatment. The father grumbled but said he would return. In further therapy, John often complained about being humiliated by his father, and made the point that family members should support one another. He then alluded to the dissension between his parents, stating that the family seemed most at peace when the father was away on one of his business trips or engaged in "other activities." The mother agreed.

At a later session, the son complained that his father had refused to support him in a problem he had with another boy during the eighth grade. The other youngster, a bully, abused and humiliated John. When John approached his father with the problem, the older man had told him it was time he learned to settle his own affairs. John became quite emotional as he recounted this episode and his father flushed during the discussion. The therapist remarked that the boy needed an older and encouraging male to make him feel capable of meeting challenges, both at home and at school, and the lack of the father's support interfered with his ability to think of himself as a potent male. Besides, John interpreted his father's refusal to help him as a rejection and a further blow to his self-esteem.

As the discussion proceeded, the father stated that he never tried to reject or humiliate his son, that in his own way, he was trying to foster independence and growth in the boy. At that point, the mother stated, "You sure haven't done a very good job of it! Of all people, you should know how much a son needs the support of his father." The father looked at her angrily and then at the floor. The therapist noted, "Perhaps you haven't been aware that you've been treating your son in much the same way that you were treated when you were growing up." With that remark, the father began to weep uncontrollably. The therapist explained that in his own conduct with John he was repeating some of the painful scenes from his own early life, but that this could change now that he recognized that he could help John, both by being a suitable male role model for the boy as well as a more contributing member of the family unit.

During this discussion between therapist and husband, the wife attempted to further humiliate the man, but the therapist interceded and suggested to her that this could be a turning point in family relatedness. The father had now become aware that he was repeating something from his own childhood and re-experiencing the pain; the mother too must recognize that she feared abusive males, and was not allowing the father to grow healthily in his appreciation and affection for their son. Unconsciously, perhaps she feared John becoming assertive, and therefore abusive.

After that session, John was excused from therapy for several weeks and the couple was seen together. The man's background in a family where the mother exercised tight control was reviewed. He grew up apprehensive of women and having doubts about his own masculinity, since there was no suitable male to support him. Similarly, they discussed the mother's earlier life, of being brought up in a family where the father and older brothers were abusive to her. A correlation was made between each of their own past lives and what happened in their marriage. A new equilibrium was established. The father began taking the wife on an occasional business trip, and they would stay an extra day "so we could be together."

The therapist also met with John in an individual session and reviewed the problems in his parents' marriage. John could not understand how their own personalities and interaction had crippled his attempts at self-assertion. The differences between assertion and aggression were discussed; assertion, the capacity for healthy self-expression and a statement of self-esteem, was clearly distinct from aggression, acting in fear, for which retaliation is anticipated. As John understood the difference between these two concepts, he became more comfortable at school and, when he called home during the week, he occasionally asked to speak with his father.

In his homosexual activity, John was usually the passive partner. This predilection was interpreted as his attempt to incorporate another man's strength much as the infant incorporates the mother's breast in a dependent setting. As these elements of sexual behavior were discussed, he became more aggressive in his homosexual activity.

Therapy with male homosexual patients must begin with an understanding of the motivation for their sexual behavior. When another man is forced into a position of inferiority, such as through oral or anal rape, the aggressor feels a sense of dominance. In fantasies about competition, the unconscious symbol of masculine success is the phallus. Strength, success, and achievement are measured in terms of phallic power; submission or failure are associated with phallic weakness. Thus, an individual who fails in expected behavior in sexual or social life may fantasize, "I am a failure, I do not feel complete as a man, I am castrated and a homosexual." Colloquial language expresses oral or anal rape: the male who is defeated by another male, or the high school student who feels the teacher gave a very hard exam, tell about being "shafted" or "reamed." The allusions to oral rape are also obvious in curse words having to do with forced sucking activity. Sexual terms may also be used to describe failure ("I got screwed"). The individual who feels defeated and humiliated may develop homosexual "panic": he feels vulnerable to a more powerful male and goes on the attack first. This is one area where homosexual interaction may become tinged with violence.

In classic literature about homosexuality, the term "latent homosexuality" is used to describe individuals who under special circumstances would engage in sex with members of the same gender. Clinically, latent homosexuals would turn out to be pseudohomosexuals—persons who feel they have failed in vocational or social areas and attempt to repair their self-image as men by incorporating the strength of another man through oral or anal sexual activity; in other situations, they attempt to subjugate another man and prove their masculinity by conquering someone of the same sex.

In therapy, when John thought about relationships with women, he felt guilty because of the memories of the "overcloseness" of his mother. Moreover, he had to deal with competitive feelings toward his father: entering a heterosexual role would make him sensitive to potential male "rivals" for the woman and such competition would stir feelings related to earlier competitive feelings toward his father.

John was successful in academic and vocational areas, and was a member of the drama club. After one of the performances, he was invited to a reception where he met a girl from a town near his own. They discovered that although they had never known each other, they had many friends in common and made arrangements to see each other again. At the therapy session following this meeting, John was quite anxious and wondered how he would conduct himself when he met the young woman. He reminded the therapist that he had dated casually in high school in groups but had never been alone with a girl. The therapist suggested that since he and the girl had many things in common, they would have no difficulty in making conversation with one another. He needn't be worried about jumping into bed at a moment's notice. John continued to date this girl, and the question of sexual involvement and commitment arose. They liked each other and were comfortable in hugging and kissing, but he feared if they became more serious, it would be too much for him.

At this point, the therapist reminded him that his homosexual behavior reflected attitudes and fears experienced in growing up in his family and interfered with his perception of himself as a competent male. The homosexual behavior was deviant and the fears would diminish in time. Going out with a girl and becoming involved with her in a more than superficial way need not stir guilt in him related to the guilt he felt about strivings toward his mother. Moreover, his anxiety was not unusual, whether or not he had been involved in homosexual activity.

This techique of interpreting in individual sessions the basis for homosexual activity is necessary. Understanding begins within the family context, but developing confidence about sexuality is an individual matter and the patient must realize that fears carried over from early life interfere with his ability to anticipate pleasurable heterosexual competence. Homosexual individuals become resistent to therapy at this point and seek every rationalization to break off female relationships. Repetitive dreams and fantasies occur which can be analyzed in terms of earlier life experiences—fear of castration, guilt about women, fear of competition, fear of failure.

Fortunately, John was successful in social and vocational areas of his life. Strength in nonsexual areas allowed him to envision himself as potent in the sexual area. These strengths in nonsexual endeavors were instrumental in helping him eventually to achieve competence in heterosexuality.

Family oriented therapy of the homosexual patient allows parents and offspring to identify the context in which the symptom arose. When the psychodynamic background of each member of the group is understood, therapy can be specific in freeing up past conflicts and defenses in all members. The parents can now lend support to the therapy and not sabotage change in the individual and in themselves.

V

When All Else Has Failed: A Dynamic New Team Approach

Carmelita Dyess Becker

Carmelita Dyess Becker is now realizing a new midlife career as secretary at the Denver Catholic Pastoral Center. She has worked in Cana programs and marriage enrichment. With her husband, she established parish-based team marriage counseling. She was also instrumental in developing, with the staff of the Family Life Services—Denver, a program for marriage counseling ministry.

I suppose if you can tune into today's disposable product syndrome, you can toss commitment away along with the paper plates and write for the popularly advertised "Do It Yourself Divorce Kit." Priced at $85.00, the divorce kit looked like a promising alternative for Bud and me ten years ago. But because we deeply believed in the sacramental and covenantal marks of our Catholic marriage, we chose to see a priest.

We turned to a priest because it was in the church that Bud and I learned our values, and we had high hopes that the teachers of our faith would help us find the answers to our dilemma. The search for help within a pastoral setting proved for us to be as painful as our relationship.

In a period of six months, we visited more than a few rectories. We took with us years of disappointment, frustration, bitterness, and anger, along with the guilt of failing God and our six children. I do not recall in any of those sessions having the priest "tune in" to our feelings. We were treated as an institution rather than two people in pain. We heard statements such as "You must put an end to this foolishness for the sake of the children," "Are you aware of your responsibility, as a married couple, to the Church," and "You will give scandal to the community," and they further added to our guilt. Bud was reminded of his selfishness, and I felt as if I were bleeding to death and being chastised for dropping blood on the carpet. One priest, however, told us something that made sense at the time. He said, "You two will never make it." We decided to follow his prophecy and call it quits.

Very soon after our decision to separate, but before we settled into a legal separation, a couple we had worked with in Pre-Cana programs invited us to join them in a weekend of personal growth. The weekend offered a group setting where married couples were encouraged to talk about "feelings." Since Bud and I did not talk the language of feelings, we thought this might be helpful for us in caring for the children after we parted. Besides it was free; so we went.

That weekend Bud and I painfully struggled through the barriers that for so long had blocked our communication. Hope began for us. Our road was not easy. The process was slow; but trained, nonprofessional lay people enabled us to see the possibility that our marriage could work. We were treated not as "one" but two unique, significant persons living in a marriage relationship. In a period of one year we were strong enough to become facilitators ourselves. What other couples had done for us, we wanted to do for couples who were in a painful relationship.

During this time Bud and I tuned into the humanness of the person and kept our distance from spiritual matters or how spirituality affected the lives of the many persons who came to the weekends. But as our scars healed enough that we were able to feel the lack of a church community in our lives and the lives of those who wanted to talk spirituality, we began to consider taking our talents to the parish. We wanted to reach those who for various reasons did not come to the weekends. We wanted to reach people in the inner city. We wanted to cooperate with the Church in healing hurting marriages.

In December of 1974, Father Tom Dowd paid us the first of many visits. That visit was in response to an invitation we had extended to Tom the previous summer when we had met him in a small town in northern Colorado. The Sunday we met Tom, we briefly discussed our ideas on teaming up with a priest to do marriage counseling in a parish setting. We hoped that when he came to Denver he would visit with us, but we did not believe circumstances would permit our meeting again, in spite of our earnestness.

Tom was assigned to St. Patrick's Church, an inner city parish, in the fall of 1975. Before he settled into his new assignment, Tom met with the staff of St. Pat's to inquire about the most outstanding needs to be met in the parish. The unanimous response he received indicated a crying need for marriage counseling. Excited with this information, Tom made his first visit to us.

As we shared our concern for marriages that evening, a new ministry opened up for Bud and me. Parish-based team marriage counseling would soon be offered at St. Patrick's parish. The concept of a three-person approach to counseling developed out of Tom's excitement over the success ratio of peer counseling he had experienced the previous year at the Hollywood Institute of Marriage and Family Counseling. In addition to the proven success of peer counseling, we strongly believed that trained married couples with a priest could successfully enable people in hurting marriages to find spiritual healing. Two sacraments, both of which call for social ministering, could witness to the parish community the real living out of Christ's message: "Feed my lambs."

Before our first counseling session, the three of us spent many hours encouraging each other to be honest with ourselves so that we would not preach, but reach out to the pain of those who trusted in us. We felt then, and we feel now, that unconditional positive regard for people enables people to grow.

For two and one-half years Tom, Bud, and I counseled every Tuesday evening. We were never short of people who wanted to find new meaning for their lives. There was a steady stream of people, because Tom acted on the belief that often pastors need to go out to people who are hurting. He calls this "recruitment." Tom is not satisfied to let that hint, "I am hurting," he hears after mass fade into the sunset. After not hearing from that person in a respectable length of time, Tom manages a home visit. And around the kitchen table he discusses the possibility of counseling at the parish. At times there has been a raised eyebrow as Tom explained our new method of counseling—that of the team approach. But in all the time we have devoted to this ministry, no one has refused to at least give us a try. Father puts himself in charge of "recruitment," and Bud and I are in charge of "groupment." These terms identify how Tom sees one of the values of our team—he gets them there and we keep them there.

A few couples have been "foot draggers," people unsure of what to expect from us. But in time they usually stop looking to Father alone for guidance and begin to tune in to Bud and me.

One of the real advantages of team counseling is that three heads are better than one or two. As one counselor is actively involved with one of the counselees, another is free to pick up on the feelings of the remaining spouse. And as a pastoral team we are free to listen in for spiritual needs along with emotional ones.

Since we are not professionals, we do not pretend to be therapists in the strictest sense of the term. We know our limitations and so do the couples we see. The first evening we meet a couple we explain our capabilities as well as our limitations and mention the possibility of referral if needed.

In our ministry we emphasize good communication, and we teach couples communication techniques. But there are no secrets, or magic formulas. What we have learned we freely offer to others. We do not ask "why." We do not try to interpret the Socratic dictum, "Know Thyself," but rather help people in their efforts to heed it.

Our method emphasizes the need for individuality, self-respect, personal responsibility, and the need for a person to become whole before two can become one in marriage.

We have made mistakes and have learned from them. Two couples we counseled have divorced, and at least two have separated. We don't know if that is our failure or success.

One thing we know for sure is that when those couples came to the rectory hurting, they were not preached at. A priest and a married couple, representing the faith community, were present to their pain, accepted them, and encouraged them to find themselves and each other, if it was at all possible.

The night of Tom's first visit with us we asked him to help us spread the concept of team counseling if he found it to be priestly. One year later Tom called the director of Family Life Services to share with him our concept of a ministry. The Director, Dr. Lewis Barbato, a psychiatrist, visited with Tom and in Dr. Barbato's words "found a pearl." Soon after that visit, Bud and I were asked to offer Dr. Barbato and his professional staff our ideas for a training program. Our efforts, experience, and dream are now a program and ministry.

Dr. Barbato has personally visited each priest who is interested in this shared ministry. It is the priest who selects couples from his parish to attend the course offered by the professional staff at the Family Life Center. Theory, technique, and practice are included in a fifty-hour course for couples who care about the sacramentality of marriage.

What does the future hold? The Family Life Center is now training men and women who have suffered the loss of their relationship to help others. Young couples are being trained to prepare other young couples for marriage. Young parents may come to the Center to learn how to parent more effectively.

Father Tom is working on establishing an inner-city pastoral counseling service and Bud and I are working with another couple and a parish priest on a program of personal-spiritual growth at the parish level.

In 1968, the two who were not even one were almost none. In 1974, those two became three. By 1978, the three had become almost 100. "Feed my lambs!"

The Valley Times-

A Final Word

Paul F. Wilczak Ph.D.

"The reign of God is like a buried treasure which a man found in a field. He hid it again, and rejoicing at his find went and sold all he had and bought that field." Mt. 13,44

The analogy between this parable and ministering to hurting families may not be immediately evident but consider:

Hurting families live out their painful existence in very ordinary settings. Their routines of life are treadmills of suffering which are gradually mistaken for the full extent of human existence from which there is no escape. This holds true until the worth of a new caring experience, a treasurable human encounter, breaks the routine. It comes from beyond the boundaries of the family. Like the treasure in the field, it can transform the lives of those who meet up with it.

Good therapy results from more than technique, more than professional competence. Its foundation is care and personal commitment. In the healing encounter a therapist's "goodness" seems to go beyond merely being a good therapist. The therapist's work expresses the reign of God among us and his other care, in a hidden way, symbolizes the care of God our Father.

Much can be learned of the concrete meaning of the theological virtues by studying the efforts of family counselors, for God is at work in their work whether they are aware of this or not. Therefore, ministers must learn from them and enter even deeper into that mirror of love which is human care. This boils down to getting involved with troubled people.

What Carmelita Dyess Becker has detailed in her chapter on pastoral marriage counseling points out the road for family ministries in the future. "We wanted to cooperate with the Church in healing hurting marriages," she said. This means learning the nature of hurt and of what helps healing and then putting this into practice in the local churches. We hope this book will stimulate creative pastoral responses by bringing problems into focus, and describing ways of dealing with them.

Questions for Reflection and Discussion

The Family Seen as a System

(See pp. 13-27)

1. What is your personal reaction to the family viewed as a system? What does it mean to think of your own family as a system?

2. What seems to be the strong and weak points of this systems approach to healing in the family?

3. What is the attitude in your community toward family therapy? How much do people know about it?

4. What are some of the implications of Dr. Kerr's perspective for ministry to families? How informed should pastors be about this view of the family?

The Role of Celebrant in Family Therapy

(See pp. 29-39)

1. How would you describe the special appropriateness of having a priest, minister, or rabbi assist in the solving of family problems? What special resources do they have to assist most families?

2. Are some of the family conflicts you have had in the past, or are having now, attributable to an imbalance of continuous and discontinuous values? In what ways are these issues conflicts between heart-reasoning and head-reasoning?

3. Can everyone become a "celebrant" in the resolution of family conflicts? What special skills are required? Does one have to be a trained therapist? Can you yourself give any examples of how "outsiders" have successfully intervened to help your own family? Have you performed that same role for other families? Do you think more should be done in this vein? What holds us back?

Family Systems Therapy: A Path to Coping

(See pp. 41-53)

1. What do you perceive as the basic insight of family systems therapy? How does thinking of your own family as a system help you?

2. Do you think family problems are brought on more by the acts of a single member or by the acts of a committee, i.e., your whole family? Why? Does your manner of dealing with problems reflect a "single culprit theory" or a "systems theory?"

3. The author discussed family vulnerability. Do you think that families today are more defenseless than those of previous times? Or are we about the same? Can you give some examples?

Family Oriented Therapy of Homosexual Behavior

(See pp. 55-67)

1. In what way does the article bring to light the manner in which all families operate? Sometimes the family is described as a "system." What is the evidence for this interpretation of family life in the case presented?

2. Do you believe that an understanding of homosexuality is important for all persons to have? Why? Many persons complain that they are bothered by the topic of homosexuality. Is this negative response something that people should try to overcome, or is it the case that the less said, the better?

3. To what extent can homosexuality respond to healing in the family?

When All Else Has Failed

(See pp. 69-76)

1. While you may not be in a program like the one in the article, do you ever see yourself helping other couples in their marriages? Do you usually think that it is none of your business? How might you help without giving the impression that you are helping?

2. What struck you most about this innovative system of helping? What is the key that makes if work?

3. How do you think one makes a judgment that certain problems demand professional help?

Suggested Readings

Ackerman, Nathan W. *Treating the Troubled Family.* New York: Basic Books, Inc., 1966.

The late author was one of the grandfather figures in the family therapy movement. Here he has presented his characteristic approach and values in a clear and practical way.

Beavers, W. Robert. *Psychotherapy and Growth: A Family Systems Perspective.* New York: Brunner/Mazel, Publishers, 1977.

This is a fundamental, even philosophical, consideration of basic issues in contemporary psychotherapy. The psychiatrist-author clarifies eight family variables which can be used to specify family health or dysfunction along a continuum. Included among the variables is the family's sense of transcendent values. An excellent, readable book.

Bowen, Murray. *Family Therapy in Clinical Practice.* New York: Jason Aronson, 1978.

This volume is a collection of articles by one of the pioneers in family therapy and the founder of a ma-

jor therapeutic school. Michael E. Kerr and Patricia H. Meyer, two of the authors contributing to *Healing in the Family,* are members of Dr. Bowen's staff at Georgetown University. The contents of the above book have been gathered from professional journals often difficult to locate. They cover a span of two decades.

Ferber, Andrew; Mendelsohn, Marilyn; and Napier, Augustus. *The Book of Family Therapy.* Boston: Houghton Mifflin Company, 1972.

One of the first in-depth anthologies on family therapy, this book retains its value. Differences among therapists are clarified and families who have been in therapy comment on how it has helped them.

Foley, Vincent D. *An Introduction to Family Therapy.* New York: Grune and Stratton, Inc., 1974.

This is a textbook-type introduction to basic concepts and issues of family therapy. There is a valuable comparing and contrasting of five key therapists: Ackerman, Bowen, Satir, Haley, and Jackson.

Guerin, Philip J. Jr., ed. *Family Therapy: Theory and Practice.* New York: Gardner Press, Inc. 1976.

A major collection of articles by some of the best known therapists practicing today.

Haley, Jay. *Problem-Solving Therapy: New Strategies for Effective Family Therapy.* San Francisco: Jossey-Bass,1976.

This is probably Haley's best book and is considered to be one of the best for persons in family therapy training. It includes the verbatim record of the

famous case Haley supervised ("A Modern Little Hans") in which a young boy's phobia of dogs was treated.

Minuchin, Salvador. *Families and Family Therapy.* Cambridge, MA: Harvard University Press, 1974.

An excellent presentation of the structural approach. Reconstructing techniques are carefully analyzed and persented in examples from work with actual families.

Minuchin, Salvador, et al. *Families of the Slums: An Exploration of Their Structure and Treatment.* New York: Basic Books, Inc. 1967.

This epoch-making book began the development of what is probably the most influential school of family therapy, the structural approach, characteristic of the Philadelphia Child Guidance Clinic. This form of therapy was developed as an alternative to the more traditional verbal type which was found to be ineffective with ghetto families. The structual approach later proved to be effective with all families.

Minuchin, Salvador, et al. *Psychosomatic Families: Anorexia Nervosa in Context.* Cambridge, MA: Harvard University Press, 1978.

The most recent, detailed presentation of the structural approach to a life-threatening family problem, the self-starvation disease. The analysis and discussion of verbatim family interviews are excellent and provide examples of structural interventions which demonstrate the effectiveness of this therapy.

Papp, Peggy, ed. *Family Therapy: Full*

Length Case Studies. New York: Gardner Press, Inc., 1977.

A valuable collection of cases by well-known skillful therapists such as Carl Whitaker and Harry Aponte. It provides examples of strategic goals and ways to achieve them.

Satir, Virginia. *Making Contact.* Millbrae, CA: Celestial Arts, 1976.

Written for nonprofessional readers as a summary of Satir's position, this book is the best introduction to her viewpoint. Its language is nontechnical and easy to follow.

Satir, Virginia; Stachowiak, James; Taschman, Harvey, A.; Tiffany, Donald, W.; et al. *Helping Families to Change.* New York: Jason Aronson, Inc., 1975.

An excellent example of Satir's therapeutic approach by way of family communication. Includes helpful exercises and a verbatim account of an actual session with a rural family.

Zuk, Gerald, H. *Process and Practice in Family Therapy.* Haverford, PA: Psychiatry and Behavioral Science Books, 1975.

An interesting and helpful book by a leading family therapist. Dr. Zuk taught his approach to Father Andrew Bambrick, who is quoted in some of the sections. The work is a valuable update of Zuk's understanding of the pathogenic relating which occurs around unresolved family conflicts.

